LOL

KNOCK KNOCK
...Who's there?

and other laugh-out-loud jokes

This edition first published in 2013 by Ginger Fox Ltd
Copyright © 2013 Ginger Fox Ltd

Published in the UK by:
Ginger Fox Ltd
Stirling House, College Road
Cheltenham GL53 7HY
United Kingdom

www.gingerfox.co.uk

Compiled by Kelly Owen
Illustrated by Mike Phillips

ISBN: 978-1-909290-07-5

10 9 8 7 6 5 4 3 2 1

Printed and bound in China.

CONTENTS

JUST
FOR
LAUGHS

Why didn't the sailors play cards?
Because the captain was
sitting on the deck.

What did Adam say on the day
before Christmas?
'It's Christmas, Eve!'

Did you hear about the man who read
a book about anti-gravity?
It was impossible to put down.

A man asked his friend,
'Have you ever gone to bed with
an ugly woman?'
His friend replied,
'No, but I've woken up with a few!'

Jesus walked into a bar and asked for a
glass of water,
which he promptly turned into wine.
'What do you think you're doing?'
yelled the barman.
Jesus replied, 'Well, I'm not paying your
prices for a glass of Sauvignon Blanc!'

How can sea captains use amphibians?
As froghorns.

Did you hear about the man who got drunk and fell asleep beside the bar?
It caused a massive delay at the ballet competition.

How did the police know that the man who'd been eaten by a shark had dandruff?
They found his head and shoulders on the beach.

I was walking in a cemetery this morning and saw a bloke hiding behind a gravestone.
'Morning,' I said.
'No,' he replied, 'just having a pee.'

'Doctor, I have a cricket ball stuck
in my ear.'
'How's that ...'
'Oh, don't you start!'

A newspaper editor went to the doctor.
'Doctor, I'm so stressed – my paper has lost
thousands of readers.'
'OK, I'll prescribe you some pills.'
'Will they help with my stress?'
'No, but they'll improve your circulation!'

'Doctor, I keep sleepwalking,' said the man.
'Try these,' said the doctor, handing
him a small box.
'Are they sleeping pills?' asked the man.
'No, they're drawing pins.
Sprinkle them on the floor next to
your bed!'

'Doctor, I can't get to sleep at night.'
'Try lying on the edge of the bed - you'll soon drop off!'

A man walked into the doctor's
with a lettuce leaf
sticking out of his ear.
'That's strange,' said the doctor.
'That's just the tip of the iceberg!'
said the man.

A man in a restaurant asked the waiter,
'How do you prepare the chicken?'
'We don't,' said the waiter,
'we just tell it straight that it's going to die!'

A man said to his friend,
'I've just been to the dentist.'
'So does your tooth still hurt?'
his friend asked.
'I don't know. He kept it.'

Did you hear about the man who had a
phobia of hurdles?
He got over it eventually.

A man went into a pet shop and
asked for a goldfish.
'Sure,' said the assistant.
'Do you want an aquarium?'
'I don't care what star sign it is,'
replied the man.

What's smelly, round and laughs?
A tickled onion.

I was doing some decorating, so I got out my stepladder.
I don't get on with my real ladder.

I found being an electrician interesting, but the work was shocking!

I rang up a local builder and said, 'I want a skip outside my house.'
'Go ahead,' he said, 'I'm not stopping you!'

Last week I replaced every window
in my house.
Then I discovered I had a crack in
my glasses.

What did the plumber say to his wife when
he wanted a divorce?
'It's over, Flo!'

A sergeant and two of his men went
into a bar.
'Would you like a game of pool?'
the sergeant asked the attractive barmaid.
'No thanks,' she replied.
'I'd rather play with your privates.'

Why did the Mexican shoot his wife?
Tequila.

When did the dentist become a
brain surgeon?
When his drill slipped.

Never, under any circumstances, take a
sleeping pill and a laxative on
the same night.

I got some new aftershave today that
smells like breadcrumbs.
All the birds love it!

How do you tickle a rich girl?
Say, 'Gucci, Gucci, Gucci!'

How many sides does a circle have?
Two: an inside and an outside.

What do you call tired army clothes?
Fatigues.

What colour is a belch?
Burple.

What did Tarzan say to his wife?
'Jane, it's a jungle out there!'

What did the alien dandelion say to the
Earth dandelion?
'Take me to your weeder!'

What did the guitar say to the musician?
'Pick on someone your own size!'

What did the boy say when his mother
poured porridge over him?
'How can you be so gruel?'

What do you call a vet with laryngitis?
A hoarse doctor.

What do you give a person with water on the brain?
A tap on the head.

What did the painter say to the wall?
'One more crack and I'll plaster you!'

What do you get when you drop a piano
down a mineshaft?
A flat miner.

What goes, 'Ha, ha, ha, plop'?
A man laughing his head off.

What do you get when you put pictures
of the kings of Russia on a flag?
The Tsar-Spangled Banner.

What does a spy do when he gets cold?
He goes under cover.

What happened to the lawyer who was
thrown out of a pub?
He was disbarred.

What is copper nitrate?
Overtime for policemen.

What is a centrifuge?
A place where 100 people can hide.

What is an electrician's favourite
Christmas carol?
'The Twelve Days of Christmas' -
because of the partridge in ampere tree.

What's a chimney sweep's most
common ailment?
The flue.

What is heaven for gamblers?
Paradise.

What jumps from cake to cake and
smells of almonds?
Tarzipan.

What part of a cemetery is best for
burying guns?
The muzzleum.

What's Irish and sits in the sun?
Paddy O'Furniture.

What's a three-season bed?
One without a spring.

What's musical and handy
in a supermarket?
A Chopin Liszt.

What's the motto of the ghouls' convention?
The morgue the merrier.

Why are there never floods in Paris?
Because the water is always l'eau.

Where did Noah keep his bees?
In the ark hives.

What's the similarity between a blacksmith
and a counterfeiter?
They're both into forgery.

Why do ambassadors never get sick?
They have diplomatic immunity.

Where did the king put his armies?
In his sleevies.

Why are meteorologists always nervous?
Their future is always up in the air.

Why did the man quit his job at the helium gas factory?
Because he didn't like being spoken to in that tone of voice.

Why did the baker have smelly hands?
Because he kneaded a poo.

What's a bigamist?
An Italian fog.

ALL CREATURES GREAT AND SMALL

What cruises along the river
at 60mph?
A motorpike with two side carps.

Two sheep were standing in a field.
One went, 'Baaaa.'
The other went,
'Damn! I was going to say that.'

What do you get when you drop boiling
water down a rabbit hole?
Hot cross bunnies.

What do you call a newly hatched beetle?
A baby buggy.

What has four legs and flies?
A dead horse.

Two fleas left a nightclub.
One turned to the other and said,
'Do you want to walk or shall we
take a dog?'

Two hedgehogs were standing
at the roadside.
'Shall we cross?' asked one.
'No way,' said the other.
'Have you seen what happened
to the zebra?'

Why aren't dogs good dancers?
Because they have two left feet.

What kind of monkey can fly?
A hot-air baboon.

What happens to ducks before
they grow up?
They grow down.

A chicken saw a duck standing by the side
of the road.
The chicken walked over to the duck
and said,
'Don't do it, mate. You'll never hear
the end of it!'

Why don't owls mate during a storm?
Because it's too wet to woo.

Why do birds fly south for the winter?
Because it's too far to walk.

Where are whales weighed?
At a whale weigh station.

Did you hear about the dog that loved
eating garlic?
His bark was worse than his bite.

Why did the chicken cross the road?
It wanted to be poultry in motion.

Why did the chicken cross
the road halfway?
Because it wanted to lay it on the line.

Why did the rubber chicken cross the road?
To stretch its legs.

Why did the sheep cross the road?
To get to the baa-baas.

Why did the turtle cross the road?
To get to the shell station.

What city has the largest
rodent population?
Hamsterdam.

The best way to catch rabbits is to hide
behind a tree and make a noise
like a lettuce.

A penguin walked into a bar and
asked the barman,
'Have you seen my brother?'
'I don't know,' said the barman.
'What does he look like?'

Why don't oysters give to charity?
Because they're shellfish.

What's worse than a bull in a china shop?
A hedgehog in a condom factory.

What happens to illegally parked frogs?
They get toad away.

What's green and red and goes round and
round at 90mph?
A frog in a blender.

What kind of bees give milk?
Boo bees.

Two slugs were slithering down the road.
As they got to the corner they came up
behind two snails.
'Oh no,' groaned one. 'Caravans!'

How do you change tyres on a duck?
With a quackerjack.

If a seagull flies over the sea, what flies
over the bay?
A bagel.

A MAN WALKS INTO A BAR ...

A man walks into a bar with a steering
wheel in his underpants.
'Is that painful?' asks the barman.
'It's driving me nuts!' the man replies.

Two ropes walk into a bar. The barman says
to them, 'Hey! We don't serve ropes in here.'
So one of the ropes leaves.
The other rope looks a bit tatty,
and the barman asks,
'Aren't you a rope too?'
To which the rope replies,
'No, I'm afraid not.'

What do you call a mushroom that runs
into a bar and buys a round of drinks for
everyone?
A fun guy.

Shakespeare walks into a bar.
'Get out,' says the barman, 'you're bard!'

A sandwich goes into a pub, walks up to the barman and says, 'Pint of lager, please.' 'Sorry mate,' says the barman, 'we don't serve food in here.'

A brain goes into a pub and says, 'Pint of lager, please.' The barman replies, 'Sorry mate, you're already out of your head.'

An Englishman, an Irishman and a Scotsman walk into a pub. The barman looks up and says, 'Is this some kind of joke?'

Four fonts walk into a bar. The barman says,
'Oi – get out! We don't want your
type in here!'

A man walks into a bar with a lump of
tarmac under his arm.
'What would you like?' asks the barman.
'A pint of lager for me' replies the man,
'and one for the road.'

A cowboy walks into a saloon bar with a
coconut-filled chocolate bar on his head.
'What's up with him?' the barman asks
one of the regulars.
'Oh, he's got a bounty on his head.'

A jump lead walks into a bar, and looks
around aggressively at the other customers.
The barman says, 'All right, I'll serve you ...
but don't start anything.'

PERFECT THE PUNCHLINE

I got pulled over by the police last night
and ordered to get out of my car.
'You're staggering!' the policeman said.
'You're not so bad-looking yourself,'
I replied.

How do you fix a woman's watch?
You don't have to. There's a clock
on the oven.

Following the theft of a truck full of toupees,
police officers were reported to be
combing the area.

Ten thousand bars of soap were stolen from a warehouse.
Police say the thieves made a clean getaway.

Why did the escaped convict saw the legs off his bed?
Because he wanted to lie low

What's the difference between a lawyer
and a herd of buffalo?
A lawyer charges more.

How can you tell if a cello is out of tune?
The bow is moving.

Why are harps like elderly parents?
They're unforgiving and hard to get in
and out of cars.

What do you get if you cross a panda
and a harp?
A bear-faced lyre.

What's the best way to tune a banjo?
With wire cutters.

Why did the mathematician turn off the
heating in his home?
So that he could be cold and calculating.

It's really difficult to find what you want on eBay. I was searching for cigarette lighters and found over 15,000 matches.

I phoned my office this morning and said, 'Sorry boss, I can't come in today.
I have a wee cough.'
He said, 'You have a wee cough?'
I said, 'Really? Cheers boss,
see you next week!'

I woke up this morning and forgot which side the sun rises. Then it dawned on me.

I put some body spray on last night, but I only managed to pull Anne Robinson.
It must have been the weakest Lynx.

A new nightclub has just opened down the road, and they're offering as much as you can drink all night for just under 20 quid. So tonight I'm going to party like it's £19.99.

I sell balloons for 10p each, or if you want them blown up it's 15p.
I've adjusted the price to allow for inflation.

What's the difference between an oral and
a rectal thermometer?
The taste!

What did the fish say when it hit the wall?
'DAM!'

Why did the traffic lights turn red?
Wouldn't you, if you had to change in the
middle of the street?

How do you catch a unique rabbit?
Unique up on it.

How do crazy people get
through the forest?
They take the psycho path.

How do you get holy water?
You boil the hell out of it.

What do Eskimos get from sitting on
the ice too long?
Polaroids.

What do you call a boomerang
that doesn't work?
A stick.

What do you call cheese that isn't yours?
Nacho cheese.

OPPOSITES
ATTRACT

Relationship Terms

1. ARGUMENTS

A woman always has the last word in any argument. Anything a man says after that is the beginning of a new argument.

2. BATHROOMS

A man has six items in his bathroom: toothbrush and toothpaste, shaving cream, razor, a bar of soap and a towel. The average number of items in the typical woman's bathroom is 337. A man would not be able to identify more than 20 of these items.

3. DRESSING UP

A woman will dress up to go shopping, water the plants, put out the bins, answer the phone or read a book. A man will dress up for weddings and funerals.

4. EATING OUT

When the bill arrives, Mike, Dave and John will each throw in £20, even though the bill is only for £32.50. None of them will have anything smaller and none will actually admit they want change back. When the girls get their bill, out come the pocket calculators.

5. FUTURE

A woman worries about the future until she gets a husband. A man never worries about the future until he gets a wife ...

6. MARRIAGE

A woman marries a man expecting he will change, but he doesn't. A man marries a woman expecting she won't change, but she does.

7. MONEY

A man will pay £2 for a £1 item he needs. A woman will pay £1 for a £2 item she doesn't need if it's on sale.

8. NATURAL

Men wake up as good-looking as when they went to bed. Women somehow deteriorate during the night.

9. NICKNAMES

If Laura, Kate and Sarah go out for lunch, they will call each other Laura, Kate and Sarah. If Mike, Dave and John go out to the pub, they will affectionately refer to each other as Fat Boy, Dickhead and Shit-for-Brains.

10. OFFSPRING

Ah, children. A mother knows all about her children. She knows about dental appointments, romances, best friends, favourite foods, secret fears, and hopes and dreams. A father is vaguely aware that some short people are living in the house.

11. SUCCESS

A successful man is one who makes more money than his wife can spend. A successful woman is one who can find such a man.

I haven't spoken to my wife in 18 months -
I don't like to interrupt her.

My credit card was stolen, but I decided
not to report it since the thief was spending
much less than my wife did.

'Doctor, I'm having trouble sleeping.'
'You need to stop taking your troubles to
bed with you,' advised the doctor.
'I would, but my wife refuses to sleep alone.'

Men who have pierced ears are better
prepared for marriage.
They've experienced pain and
bought jewellery.

How do most men define marriage?
An expensive way to get your laundry
done for nothing.

Why do men fart more than women?
Because women won't shut up long enough
to build up the pressure.

It's not true that married men live longer
than single men. It only *seems* longer.

A man met a genie. The genie told him he
could ask for whatever he wanted, and
would get it, but his mother-in-law would
get double whatever he asked for. The man
thought for a moment and said,
'OK, give me a million pounds and beat me
till I'm half-dead.'

What do a hurricane, a tornado, a fire and a divorce have in common?
They are four ways you can lose your house.

Two men were admiring a famous model. 'Still,' said one, 'if you take away her beautiful hair, her pert breasts, her smouldering eyes and her stunning figure, what are you left with?'
'My wife,' the other replied.

A man was complaining to a friend: 'I had it all - money, a beautiful house, a big car, the love of a beautiful woman - and then, BAM! It was all gone.'
'What happened?' asked his friend.
'My wife found out ...'

Did you hear about the couple who met in
a revolving door?
They're still going round together.

What's the difference between a girlfriend
and a wife?
45lb.

What's the difference between a boyfriend
and a husband?
45 minutes.

If all brides are beautiful, where the hell do ugly wives come from?

'Doctor, my wife has lost her voice. How can I help her get it back?'
'Try coming home at 3 o'clock in the morning.'

What do train sets and breasts have in common?
They're intended for children, but it's usually men who end up playing with them.

How many men does it take to open a beer?
None. It should be opened by the time she brings it to you.

Top 10 Rejection Lines Given by Women

10. I think of you as a brother.
(You remind me of that inbred banjo-playing geek in 'Deliverance'.)

9. There's a slight difference in our ages.
(I don't want to do my dad.)

8. I'm not attracted to you in 'that' way.
(You're the ugliest man I've ever laid eyes on.)

7. My life is too complicated right now.
(I don't want you spending the whole night here as you'll hear the phone calls from all the other guys I'm seeing.)

6. I've got a boyfriend.
(I prefer my male cat and a tub of Ben & Jerry's.)

5. I don't date men where I work.
(I wouldn't date you in the same 'solar system', let alone the same building.)

4. It's not you, it's me.
(It's you.)

3. I'm concentrating on my career.
(Even something as boring and unfulfilling as my job is better than dating you.)

2. I'm celibate.
(I've sworn off men – but only men like you.)

1. Let's be friends.
(I want you to stay around so I can tell you in excruciating detail about all the other men I meet and have sex with. It's that male perspective thing.)

How to Shower Like a Woman

Take off clothing and place it in sectioned laundry basket according to lights and darks.

Walk to bathroom wearing long dressing gown. If you see husband on the way, cover up any exposed areas.

Look at your womanly physique in the mirror – make mental note to do more sit-ups, leg-lifts, etc.

Get in the shower. Use face cloth, arm cloth, leg cloth, long loofah, wide loofah and pumice stone. Wash your hair once with cucumber and sage shampoo with 43 added vitamins. Wash your hair again to make sure it's clean.

Condition your hair with grapefruit mint conditioner. Wash your face with crushed apricot facial scrub for 10 minutes until red. Wash entire rest of body with ginger nut and jaffa cake body wash.

Rinse conditioner off hair. Shave armpits and legs. Turn off shower.

Wipe down all wet surfaces and spray mould spots with bathroom cleaner. Get out of shower. Dry with towel the size of a small country. Wrap hair in super-absorbent towel.

Return to bedroom wearing long dressing gown and towel on head. If you see husband on the way, cover up any exposed areas.

How to Shower Like a Man

Take off clothes while sitting on the edge of the bed and leave them in a pile.

Walk naked to the bathroom. If you see wife on the way, shake your willy at her making the 'woo-woo' sound.

Look at your manly physique in the mirror. Admire the size of your willy and scratch your bum.

Get in the shower. Wash your face. Wash your armpits.
Blow your nose in your hands and let the water rinse them off.
Fart and laugh at how loud it sounds in the shower.
Spend majority of time washing willy and surrounding area.
Wash your bum, leaving those coarse bum hairs stuck on the soap. Wash your hair. Make a 'shampoo mohawk'. Pee.
Rinse off and get out of shower.

Partially dry off. Fail to notice the water that's all over the floor, because the shower curtain was hanging outside the bath the whole time. Admire willy size in mirror again.

Leave the shower curtain open, the wet mat on the floor, and the light and fan on.

Return to bedroom with towel around waist. If you pass wife, pull off towel, shake willy at her and make the 'woo-woo' sound again. Throw wet towel on bed.

What reduces a woman's sex drive by
90%? Wedding cake.

What should you give a woman who
has everything?
Penicillin.

OVER
THE HILL

Intelligence Test

As we age, it is important that we keep mentally alert. Below is a simple way to gauge your loss or non-loss of intelligence. So, sit back and relax. Answer each question quickly to get the most accurate result. You may begin ...

1. What do you put in a toaster?
Answer: Bread. If you said 'toast', then give up now and go and do something else. Try not to hurt yourself. If you said 'bread', proceed to question 2.

2. Say 'silk' five times. Now spell 'silk'.
What do cows drink?
Answer: Cows drink water. If you said 'milk', please do not attempt the next question. Your brain is obviously overstressed and may even overheat. It may be that you need to content yourself with reading something more appropriate, such as 'Spot the Dog'. If you said 'water', proceed to question 3.

3. If a red house is made from red bricks and a blue house is made from blue bricks and a pink house is made from pink bricks and a black house is made from black bricks, what is a greenhouse made from?
Answer: A greenhouse is made from glass. If you said 'green bricks', what are you still doing reading these questions? If you said 'glass', proceed to question 4.

4. If the hour hand on a clock moves half a degree every minute, then how many degrees will it move in one hour?

Answer: 30 degrees. If you said '360 degrees' or anything other than 30 degrees, then congratulations on getting this far but you are now obviously out of your depth. Turn in your pencil and exit the room. Everyone else proceed to the final question.

5. (Without using a calculator.) You are driving a bus from London to Milford Haven in Wales.

In London, 17 people get on the bus.

In Reading, six people get off the bus and nine people get on.

In Swindon, two people get off and four get on.

In Cardiff, 11 people get off and 16 people get on.

In Swansea, three people get off and five people get on.

In Carmarthen, six people get off and three get on.

You then arrive at Milford Haven.

What was the name of the bus driver?

Answer: Oh, for goodness sake! It was YOU – read the first line!

Symptoms of Being Over 35

1. You get more excited about having a roast on a Sunday than going clubbing.

2. You stop dreaming of becoming a professional footballer and start dreaming of having a son who might instead.

3. Before throwing the local paper away, you look through the property section.

4. Before going out anywhere, you ask what the parking is like.

5. Instead of laughing at the innovations catalogue that falls out of the newspaper, you suddenly see both the benefit and the money-saving potential of a plastic winter cover for your garden bench and an electronic mole repellent for the lawn.

6. You start to worry about your parents' health.

7. You become powerless to resist the lure of self-assembly furniture.

8. You always have enough milk in.

9. While flicking through the TV channels, you happen upon 'Time Team' with Tony Robinson. You get drawn in.

10. When sitting outside a pub you become envious of their hanging baskets.

The good news about midlife is that the glass is still half-full. Of course, the bad news is that it won't be long before your teeth are floating in it.

The most frustrating thing about getting older is that every time you see an expensive antique, you remember one just like it you once threw away.

By the time a man is old enough to read a woman like a book,
he's too old to start a library.

By the time you're wise enough to watch your step,
you're too old to go anywhere.

HAVE YOU EVER WONDERED?

Hypothetically speaking ...

1. If man evolved from monkeys and apes, why do we still have monkeys and apes?

2. What if there were no hypothetical questions?

3. How is it possible to have a civil war?

4. If the police arrest a mime artist, do they tell him he has the right to remain silent?

5. One nice thing about egotists: they don't talk about other people.

6. Do infants enjoy infancy as much as adults enjoy adultery?

7. If a parsley farmer is sued, can they garnish his wages?

8. If you try to fail, and succeed, which have you done?

9. If you spin an oriental man in a circle three times, does he become disoriented?

10. Can an atheist get insurance against acts of God?

11. If one synchronised swimmer drowns, do the rest drown too?

Don't take life so seriously ...

1. Save the whales. Collect the whole set.

2. A day without sunshine is like, night.

3. On the other hand, you have different fingers.

4. 42.7% of all statistics are made up on the spot.

5. 99% of lawyers give the rest a bad name.

6. I feel like I'm diagonally parked in a
parallel universe.

7. Honk if you love peace and quiet.

8. Remember, half the people you know
are below average.

9. Depression is merely anger without enthusiasm.

10. The early bird may get the worm, but the second
mouse gets the cheese.

11. I drive way too fast to worry about cholesterol.

12. Support bacteria. They're the only culture some people have.

13. Monday is an awful way to spend 1/7 of your week.

14. A clear conscience is usually the sign of a bad memory.

15. Change is inevitable, except from vending machines.

16. Plan to be spontaneous tomorrow.

17. Always try to be modest, and be proud of it!

18. If you think nobody cares, try missing a couple of payments.

19. How many of you believe in telekinesis? Raise my hand ...

20. Why do psychics have to ask you for your name?

HE WHO LAUGHS LAST

The World of Sport

The sport of choice for unemployed people is ten-pin bowling.

The sport of choice for maintenance staff is football.

The sport of choice for office workers is cricket.

The sport of choice for line managers is tennis.

The sport of choice for middle management is golf.

The sport of choice for company directors is squash.

Conclusion: the higher you rise in the corporate structure, the smaller your balls become.

Council Complaint Letters

1. My bush is really overgrown round the front and my back passage has fungus growing in it.

2. He's got this huge tool that vibrates the whole house and I just can't take it anymore.

3. It's the dog's mess that I find hard to swallow.

4. I want some repairs done to my cooker as it has backfired and burnt my knob off.

5. I wish to complain that my father hurt his ankle very badly when he put his foot in the hole in his back passage.

6. And their 18-year-old son is continually banging his balls against my fence.

7. I wish to report that tiles are missing from the outside toilet roof. I think it was bad wind the other night that blew them off.

8. My lavatory seat is cracked. Where do I stand?

9. Will you please send someone to mend the garden path. My wife tripped and fell on it yesterday and now she is pregnant.

10. I request permission to remove my drawers in the kitchen.

11. 50% of the walls are damp, 50% have crumbling plaster and 50% are plain filthy.

12. The toilet is blocked and we cannot bath the children until it is cleared.

13. Will you please send a man to look at my water. It is a funny colour and not fit to drink.

14. I want to complain about the farmer across the road. Every morning at 6.00am his cock wakes me up and it's now getting too much for me.

15. The man next door has a large erection in the back garden which is unsightly and dangerous.

16. I am a single woman living in a downstairs flat and would you please do something about the noise made by the man on top of me every night.

17. I have had the clerk of works down on the floor six times but I still have no satisfaction.